THE SANCTUARY OF THE SOUL

Selected Writings of THOMAS KELLY

Upper Room Spiritual Classics — Series 1

Selected, edited, and introduced by
Keith Beasley-Topliffe

UPPER
ROOM BOOKS
NASHVILLE

Unless otherwise designated, Scripture quotations are from the King James Version.

Art direction: Michele Wetherbee
Interior design and layout: Nancy Cole

First Printing: October 1997 (5)

Excerpts from *A Testament of Devotion* by Thomas R. Kelly. Copyright 1941 by Harper & Row Publishers, Inc. Renewed 1969 by Lois Lael Kelly Stabler. New introduction Copyright (c) 1992 by HarperCollins Publishers, Inc. Reprinted by permission of HarperCollins Publishers, Inc.

Excerpts from *The Eternal Promise* by Thomas Kelly. Copyright (c) 1966 by Richard M. Kelly. (Copyright (c) renewed 1994 by Richard M. Kelly. Reprinted by permission of HarperCollins Publishers, Inc.

Excerpt on pages 60–64 from the Friends United Press edition of *The Eternal Promise* is reprinted with permission of Friends United Press of Richmond, Indiana, copyright 1966.

Excerpts from *Reality of the Spiritual World* by Thomas Kelly. Copyright 1942 by Pendle Hill Publications, Wallingford, Pennsylvania.

Library of Congress Cataloging-in-Publication Data

Kelly, Thomas R. (Thomas Raymond), 1893–1941.
    [Selections. 1997]
    The sanctuary of the soul : selected writings of Thomas Kelly / selected, edited, and introduced by Keith Beasley-Topliffe.
        p. cm. — (Upper Room spiritual classics. Series 1)
      ISBN 0-8358-0829-7 (pbk.)
    1. Spiritual life — Society of Friends. 2. Society of Friends — Doctrines. I. Beasley-Topliffe, Keith. II. Title. II. Series.
BX7738.K452 1997   96-12531
248.4'896 — dc21   CIP

Printed in the United States of America

TABLE OF CONTENTS

New Fellowship

50 Θ's invading Love ⟹ new relationship w/ some humans
→ togetherness, love, sharing

51 centered & grounded in X ⟹ drawn to others likewise

52 . amazingly united w/ others in X

Opening to the World

53 joyful submission of one's all to Θ

54 look thru pain to see Eternal Lover → giving us a tender spirit

55 world's pain is ours; only bearable w/ peace, power
& victory

Seeds of Awareness, Springs of Hope

56 bearing seeds through suffering

57 take awakened seed of X w/ us through suffering ⟹ hope
⟹ growth ⟹ refuge for many

58 seed of X in all: humble people bear the seed of hope

59 w/in us living X is formed - hope of the world

Special Concerns

60 particularization of my resp.; each has a few specific concerns

61 each of us has special tasks → life simplified, ordered,
& organized

62 each a few particularized social concerns - not all things
simplification & coordination - our special issues/missions

Royal Blindness

63 focus on Θ, solely love Θ

64 quiet resting of will in Θ; indifferent to self-fortunes

65 all of self willed into Θ - complete dedication

66 become obedient unto death

67 Θ possessed channels → flow creative Love, Θ-enthralled

INTRODUCTION

Mystical experience is not only for a select few saints, sealed away in convents or monasteries from everyday life. It can come to any Christian, a gift of God's grace. The message that all Christians should look for God within, as an Inner Light, has been the message of the Society of Friends — the Quakers — for more than three centuries. In our own century, one of the greatest witnesses to God's taking hold of a life was Thomas Raymond Kelly, a Quaker professor of philosophy. During the three years between God's light bursting into a time of darkness and his death, Kelly produced a group of essays and speeches that quickly became classics of the spiritual life.

Kelly speaks from his own depth of experience, but with a clarity that comes from years of theological and philosophical study. While giving glimpses of the heights of Christian devotion, he also gives very practical advice for beginners in prayer. He emphasizes the link between mystical experience and service that relieves human suffering. He would be shocked by those who see spirituality and social action as a choice rather than a unity.

KELLY'S WORLD

Thomas Kelly's times are close enough to our own to require little introduction. His language, though, is rooted in the Quaker tradition. To understand his terminology and references, it is important to learn something about the Society of Friends (also called Quakers).

The Society of Friends grew out of the experiences of George Fox, who was born in Fenny Drayton, England, in 1624. As he grew up, he was very interested in religion and read the Bible diligently. He found little of Gospel simplicity or devotion in the Christians he saw around him, not even in the clergy. He traveled around England, seeking someone who could help him grow closer to God. During this time he probably came into contact with some of the mystical groups in England such as the Seekers or the Family of Love. In the late 1640s, a series of insights or "openings" came to him. Some of these are described in one of the selections that follow. He felt himself called to be a religious reformer, to rid the church of dependence on ancient symbols and external authority in favor of the direct experience of the Holy Spirit, or the Inner Light. (Kelly also refers to this experience as the Presence or the *Shekinah*, the Hebrew word for the abiding presence of God.) He was particularly critical of preachers who knew God only in theory, not through their own experience. His criticism extended to "steeple-houses" and use of songs in worship. Quaker worship emphasized silent prayer until someone was prompted by the Spirit to share some word with the assembly.

Fox's attacks on traditional religion met with strong counterattacks, including prosecution for blasphemy. At one defense, he told the judge that he ought to tremble before God, leading the judge to call him a Quaker, a nickname that stuck and was eventually embraced. Fox himself called his movement first the Children of the Light and later the Society of Friends. In 1652, a number of Seeker societies were "convinced" by meeting with Fox and joined him. The term *convincement* became the Quaker equivalent of conversion or conviction. Robert Barclay, a Scotsman, was "convinced" in 1666 and became the first important interpreter of the Quaker vision when he wrote *Apology for the True Christian Divinity, as the same is held forth and preached by the people, Called, in scorn, Quakers.* Another important "convincement" was that of William Penn in 1667. Penn and other Quakers bought proprietary rights to the colonies of New Jersey and what became Pennsylvania. Penn himself came to America to help found Philadelphia in 1682. Fox had already visited the colonies in 1671–73, visiting Quakers from the Carolinas to New England. George Fox died in 1691.

Over the next two centuries, the Quakers who had moved westward with the frontier began to resemble their Protestant neighbors. They had designated preachers and worship not too different from those of other Protestants. Eastern Quakers, particularly those in Pennsylvania and New Jersey, stayed closer to the old ways. Thomas Kelly grew up among the western Quakers.

The Society of Friends is organized in a structure of Meetings. The local society, or perhaps a few, met monthly for business as a Monthly Meeting.

This was related to a regional Quarterly Meeting and a much larger Yearly Meeting. There is one Yearly Meeting for all of England, another for all of Germany (which Kelly attended in 1924–25 and 1938). There are several Yearly Meetings in the United States.

KELLY'S LIFE

Thomas Kelly was born on a farm near Chillicothe, Ohio, on June 4, 1893. His parents, Carlton and Madora Kelly, were active Quakers, as had been their ancestors for several generations. He was only four years old when his father died at the age of thirty-three. Six years later, Madora Kelly moved the family to Wilmington, Ohio, to provide better educational opportunities for her children, Tom and his older sister, Mary. In 1913, Thomas Kelly graduated from Wilmington College, a Quaker school, with a degree in chemistry. He then attended Haverford College, near Philadelphia, where he earned a second bachelor's degree. More important, he met Rufus Jones, the great Quaker theologian and historian. Jones awakened an interest in philosophy that changed Kelly's life. Jones later recalled Kelly saying, "I am just going to make my life a miracle!"

Now began a long period of searching for a life's work. He taught science and English at a prep school in Canada. Feeling called to missionary work in Japan, he entered Hartford Theological Seminary in 1916. Once there, he abandoned missionary plans in favor of ministry in the United States. He also met

Lael Macy, the daughter of a Congregational minister, whom he married in 1919. First, though, came World War I. Kelly volunteered to work for the YMCA canteens near training camps in England but he was disappointed to find little opportunity for Christian witness with the soldiers. Instead, he found open hostility to Quaker pacifism in a nation at war. He soon returned home and resumed his studies.

In the fall of 1919, Kelly began two years as a teacher of Bible and philosophy at Wilmington College. Then he returned to Hartford for a doctorate and served as pastor of a nondenominational church. He received his Ph.D. in 1924. After a little more than a year serving with the American Friends Service Committee in Germany, the Kellys moved to Richmond, Indiana, where Kelly taught philosophy at Earlham College. His daughter Lois was born there in 1928. In 1930, he took a leave of absence to study at Harvard under Alfred North Whitehead and Clarence I. Lewis. He was convinced that a second doctorate from Harvard would crown his quest for academic excellence. Although he taught one year at Wellesley College, he was unable to find a permanent position in the East, and so returned to Earlham in 1932. He continued to work on his dissertation. Meanwhile, his health deteriorated. Stress brought on "woozy spells," which left his mind blank and his body exhausted. He had trouble with kidney stones in the early months of 1934, followed by what appeared to be a nervous breakdown in December. In 1935, having finished his dissertation, he took another leave from Earlham to teach at the University of Hawaii. There he had a chance for more direct encounters with Oriental philosophies. There, also, his son Richard was born in 1936. That summer the Kellys returned to the mainland, but not to Earlham: Kelly had been hired to teach at Haverford. In the fall of 1937, Kelly went to Harvard for the oral defense of his dissertation. There he had one of his woozy spells, and not only failed, but was barred from returning for another try.

Kelly was plunged into deepest despair. But sometime in the last months of 1937, a change came over him. He felt God's presence breaking into his life, giving him a new power, a new authority. His colleague Douglas Steere wrote, "He moved toward adequacy. A fissure in him seemed to close, cliffs caved in and filled up a chasm, and what was divided grew together within him." When he spoke, it was from experience, not theory. Lectures he was asked to give "wrote themselves." In 1938, Kelly was asked to make a short visit to Germany, to see what was happening to Quakers in Hitler's Third Reich. On his return he continued to teach at Haverford and accept various opportunities to speak. He began planning to publish some of his speeches and essays in a short book. On January 17, 1941, he told his wife, "Today will be the greatest day of my life." That evening he died of a sudden heart attack. He was forty-seven years old.

FURTHER READING

All the printed works from Thomas Kelly's mature period appear in *A Testament of Devotion* (Harper & Row), *The Eternal Promise* (Harper & Row and Friends United Press), and *Reality of the Spiritual World* (Pendle Hill). The first two are available in paperback. The third is a pamphlet available directly from Pendle Hill. *Thomas Kelly: A Biography* (Harper & Row) is by Richard M. Kelly, Thomas Kelly's son, and is the principal source for the biographical information above. *A Testament of Devotion* also includes a "Biographical Memoir" by Douglas Steere, who edited that collection.

For further information about Quakers, *The Faith and Practice of the Quakers* by Rufus M. Jones (Friends United Press) is the classic introduction. The journals of George Fox and of John Woolman, a New Jersey Quaker who lived just before the American Revolution, are available in a number of editions. Kelly refers frequently to their lives in the selections that follow.

Other important sources for Kelly include Meister Eckhart, a fourteenth-century German whose works are available in several editions including two volumes from Paulist Press, and Brother Lawrence, whose *The Practice of the Presence of God* is also available in several editions.

NOTE ON THE TEXTS

All selections are taken from the works listed above, with the exception of the two letters, which correct and expand on transcriptions in the biography. The selections have been edited slightly due to concerns for inclusive language that have emerged since Kelly's day. Some have also been slightly abridged. Most began as talks to specific groups and retain the informal style of direct address.

EXPERIENCING THE PRESENCE

From a letter to Lael Kelly, August 16, 1938,
in Kelly Papers, Haverford College

*After spending some time with Quakers in Nazi Germany,
Kelly crossed the German-French border to Strasbourg so
that he could write home without fear of censorship. In a
long letter, he describes the effects of repression on all
Germans and especially on the Jews, urging that that section
of the letter be passed around. Then he turns to a more
personal account of God's working in his life. This selection
is based on a transcript of the letter prepared by Kelly's
grandson, Paul Kelly, when he was a student at Haverford
College.*

This summer has *opened up* what was already
opening up before, a new sense of unreserved
dedication of oneself to a life of childlike dedication
to God. This comes not out of the feeling that one has
of having looked into the *awful depths* of human woe,
overwhelming as that is. What I want to say does not
grow out of any specific external influence—it seems
to grow out of an *internal influence*, which is so over-
mastering that I can only recognize it as God working within me. Last winter you know I was much
shaken by the experience of Presence—something
that I did not seek, but that *sought me*. It was that
which underlies the lecture on the Eternal Now.
When we read it first, that evening together, when

Jack Cadbury and Jack Carter were with us,
you said you understood the second lecture on
Symbolism, but not the first on the Eternal Now. But
this is the *real root*. And the work here this summer,
or, *in the midst of* the work here this summer, has
come an increased sense of *being laid hold on* by a
Power, a gentle, loving, but awful Power. And it
makes one *know* the reality of God at work in the
world. And it takes away the old self-seeking, self-
centered self, from which selfishness I have laid
heavy burdens on you, dear one. Help me, sweet-
heart, to become more like a little child—not proud
of learning, not ambitious for self, but emptied of
these things, and guided by that amazing Power,
which is so gentle. Yet, in the last analysis, you cannot help me; except by *understanding*, and further-
more, by *coming with me*, so far as you find it to be
your way. We have been *so* hardened, so *crusted*, so
worldly-wise. I have been *so self-seeking*, and *on the
surface* you have let experiences of Father Macy, and
Clarence Pickett's teaching, and my weakness,
sharpen you. I see my way now to a richer life of
serenity and childlike faith and joy. Come with me, if
you see this way. You need not talk much about it. I
blather on too easily. But Mother Macy must have
found it, for the fruits were to be seen in her life. I
have been *far from this way*. Now I feel I must come
home. In many ways you have always been nearer
home than I. But I *long* for companionship now, in
this area. And help me, dear one, to grow into that
kind of self-forgetful devoted life that Mother Macy

had. Don't think I am talking now in a sudden spell of emotion. It is a maturing of the Spirit that comes, sometimes slowly, but sometimes in *overwhelming spurts*. I shall, no doubt, fall far below what I should. So do we all. But let us keep close to the central intention, and the central life. The phrase *child of God* has been growing on me this summer, and amazing depths seem to lie in it. Help me, dearest, to be one. It doesn't involve complicated thinking, it just involves consecrated living, and the sensitiveness of a child to the Leading Hand. Dear one, I hope I have made myself plain. Let us both, together, find the little child within us. It doesn't mean any great overturn of *outer* life, so far as I can see. But it involves a subtler change, of inner sweetening and power, and joy and peace. I seem at last to have *been given* peace. It is amazing.

Now I have said enough, darling. Reread this page and a half several times, not only with the head, but with the heart.

Your own devoted.
Husband.

 # AMAZING
SOULS

From a letter to Lael Kelly, August 31, 1938,
in Kelly Papers, Haverford College

In this letter, Kelly writes about some of the people he has met in Germany, ordinary people with "giant souls." After opening greetings and expressions of concern for the burden he has placed on his wife by going off to Germany, Kelly gets quickly to his main subject. The lecture he mentions is The Richard Cary Lecture, given in early August. This transcription is taken directly from the original letter.

I have never had such a soul-overturning summer or period as this. Every day has brought *amazing* experiences, or acquaintance with people who have stirred me to the depths. It is not merely heroism, it is depth of consecration, simplicity of faith, beauty in the midst of poverty or suffering, that *shames* us. I have met some *giant* souls, and I must tell you about them in peace, and at length later. And one *can't* be the same again. I seem to speak in general terms, but the details are long and striking.

One thing I have learned, or feel so overwhelmingly keenly, is the real pain of suffering *with* people. Sometimes it is suffering of a physical, financial kind; sometimes of a spiritual kind, as with the present family, baffled, no outlet, no hope, no point to life, *no chance to help others bear the burdens of life* (the consequences would be serious).

And with some here I have found all the power of apostolic days in the early church. And I have found mystics of a very normal sort. Yesterday in Stuttgart I stayed over a day in order to see a workman, with black fingernails. But he knew the depths of religious experience, and we talked together, and had our arms around each other in sheer joy to find each other. He can't even speak good German, but we talked together about my lecture for spring, and he helped me! Darling, there's something *real* going on, deeper than I've been going. And oh, how glad I am to have something of it.

The family here have just asked if we three might not have a twenty-minute *Andacht* [devotion] together before I take them out to supper.

I have never had such a sense of being led as in the past few days. I have stayed with a family the man of which is like a little child, simple-minded (perhaps from war injuries) but of amazing simple trust and devotion. The sophisticated modernism and superior attitudes we meet are all gone, here, in these groups, and one seems to feel the bare knuckles of reality, or the enveloping, warming power of love, the Love of God.

An amazing little midget of a woman named Lydia Neubrand has been staying with the family part of the time. She took me around yesterday. She is a *beam* of sunshine—with a most tragic history! And this morning, as I was lying in bed, thinking about Baensch and the horrible situation, and trying to be clear what we should do for him, she came in—

the freedom here in such things is quite new to me!—and she sat on the edge of the bed, and wiped my eyes and comforted me like a mother! She even put her cheeks down against mine, but it was in a wholly impersonal, self-forgetful, spontaneous way! And we talked about the love of God and the bearing of one another's sufferings. What an amazing depth of soul! And I have met even greater souls, men and women who have stirred me with their Christlikeness or their simple trust or their deep insights or their intuitive flashes. One woman wants to write to me, but will not do it until *you* are wholly clear on the matter—that is, write about such experiences of spirit as have come to me or to her. Also, in a purely genuine spirit of love toward you she took off a lovely pendant and gave it to me [to] give to you. These things sound strange and almost fantastic and unreal. But something of the wonder of apostolic power and serenity and peace in suffering is taking place here, and I have found life's dimensions opened up amazingly. One Frenchman I met is one of the most profound mystics I have met. The amazing life of inner spirit which he has makes me leap for joy. For something of the same sort has been happening to me, and I have been just plowed down to depths I've never known before. I think the lecture opened up the springs of hearts to me and it in truth has had an enormous effect upon *me* as well. One doesn't *talk about* the Eternal Life until one has it shadowing over one. But such has come in [an] amazing way! I can't tell it fully, but I know you'll understand how deeply

I speak. That's why I wrote from Strasbourg as I did.
I had there an amazing impulsion to pray for a
certain couple, or triangle, in a tangled marriage
relation. I've found myself several times in such
rapport with people as to know their thoughts, and
they mine, without any exchange of words. No, I
haven't gone crazy, I've heard in books of such phe-
nomena, but never before have they come as direct
experience. And they are so amazing in their reality
and revelation of the active life of God in the world
that I just can't shrug my shoulders and say, in a
smart-aleck American fashion, How come? You'll
understand more, as time goes on. But I make no
claims for the future. I know that now such an
amazing series of "openings" and experiences have
come as are wholly unexpected, profound, and life-
renovating. I *do so* want to live out to the full the
consequence of such an amazing rich set of *gifts* from
an amazingly abundant hand. And I have come to
such amazingly close *innere Verbundenheit* (inner close
relations on a religious plane) with several that I
must keep up a heavy correspondence for a long long
time, as a consequence of this summer. This, not
merely to help *them*, but fully as much to be helped
by them. Certainly Johannes Lehmann (the amazing
laboring man with the black fingernails) and I
must keep up some correspondence. And Frau Else
Kappes, who comes amazingly near to being a
Christlike incarnation of love (she is the one who
gave me the pendant for you—you must write her a
dear letter). And Marius Grout, the Frenchman in

Havre who speaks my language, but more beauti-
fully—we must write from time to time.

Now I must stop, dear One. Love to you all.
And I'm on my way to you.

Your own,
Tom.

◈ RUNNING AWAY TO GOD

From "Secret Seekers" in *The Eternal Promise*

This speech was given to an unknown group in 1940 and later printed in Motive. *After affirming that there are still many souls who secretly hunger for God, Kelly speaks of how they might find God.*

Someone has said of Saint Francis that when a young man, as other young men run away to see the world, so he ran away to God. But how can we run away to God? What direction shall we run?

A few weeks ago a young college man, an athlete, sat in my office and we talked of this amazing Center, this life that is hid with Christ in God. And as I tried to tell him something of what God in His graciousness had shown of Himself to me, he said, "Gee, I'd like to find a God like that!" And I thought I almost heard the words of Job, speaking on behalf of humankind, "Oh, that I knew where I might find him."

What direction shall we run, if we would run away to God? I can only answer, He is *within* you already. Seek Him in the very deeps of your souls. But you say, "I thought we were to seek Him in the Bible." I should reply, He is not in the Bible, as such. For the Bible, as such, is a book, and words; and what you want is not a book but a living God; not words, but the *Word*, the Living Word. It is not the words of a book, but the Living Word who animated and owned those writers who wrote the Bible, that we crave. "As the hart panteth after the water brooks, so panteth my soul after thee, O God." The Book points beyond itself, to Him who has been found by its writers. And because He is already in the deeps of your own souls, these words of the Bible are made living and vivid to you. Read your Bibles, but *that isn't being religious.* Read your Bibles, and feel your way back into that Source and Spring of Life that bubbled up in the Bible-writers. And you'll find that Source and Spring of Life bubbling up *within you also.* And you'll find yourself in deep fellowship with these writers, because your life and theirs go back into the same Living Spring. It is as Robert Barclay says. The Scriptures are not the Fountain, but a declaration of the Fountain. And it is into that Fountain itself that we would step, when the angel troubles the waters, and be healed.

What direction shall we run, if we would run away to God? Some of you may say, "I shall seek Him in nature, in its beauty and its power, in its storm-tossed fury and the quiet of the forests and golden glow of sunsets." And I should reply, Yes. He comes upon us many times, in these settings, on a mountain top, at twilight, and God's Presence seems very real in those precious moments. But He is *more* than nature. And He whom we find in Nature is He who is behind and beneath and *upholding* nature. And remember, we are part of that Nature, and He is equally behind and beneath and upholding *us*, as well as the mountains and the stars. We are led back behind nature to the Source and Fountain of Nature, welling up *within* us, welling up *beyond* us in the sunset. And it is because He is *within* us that Nature *beyond* us is revealed as a companion of our inner souls. For we and Nature go back into the same creative Life. Immediacy, vivid immediacy in that Life of the Universe, is what we seek. Not in the earthquake, not in the whirlwind, not in the fire, but in a still small voice that we all have heard within us is God most immediately to be found.

What direction shall we run, if we would run away to God? Some of you may say, "I shall go into the city slums, into the war-stricken areas, into work with sharecroppers and dispossessed miners. And in the world's sufferings I shall find God." And I would reply, Yes, many have found Him in these settings and scenes of squalor and tragedy. But He whom you seek *is already there in the midst of the suffering*, bearing its load, before you ever became a bearer of the world's suffering. It is because God was already speaking within you that you went to share the burden.

It is this Inner Witness, this Inner Light, that grows brighter, in fellowship with Scripture writers, in fellowship with nature, in fellowship with service and suffering.

And now I want to let you in on a secret. How can you be sure there is a God to be found at the other end of the search? Because He has *already* been showing Himself to you, in your very impulse to seek

Him. Did you start the search for Him? He *started you* on the search for Him, and lovingly, anxiously, tenderly guides you to Himself. You knock on heaven's gate, because He has already been standing at the door and knocking within you, disquieting you and calling you to arise and seek your Father's house. It is as Saint Augustine says: He was within, and we mistakenly sought Him without. Within us all is a slumbering miracle, a latent Christ, a Light, a Power, and immediacy with God. To find this "indwelling Christ" actively, dynamically working within us, is to find the secret that Jesus wanted to give to people. It isn't a matter of *believing* in the Inner Light, it is a matter of *yielding your lives* to Him. It is a matter of daily, hourly going down into the *Shekinah* of the soul, in that silence; find yourselves continually recreated, and realigned and corrected again and again from warping effects of outer affairs. It is having a *Center* of creative power and joy and peace and creation within you.

⊡ EXPERIENCING GOD IN OUR LIVES

From "Excerpts from The Richard Cary Lecture"
in *The Eternal Promise*

*The Richard Cary Lecture, which Kelly gave at the German
Yearly Meeting in August 1938, is an expansion of his essay
"The Eternal Now and Social Concern," which can be
found in* A Testament of Devotion. *Here, he talks about
how God breaks into human lives.*

The experience is of an <u>invasion from</u> beyond,
of an Other who in gentle power breaks in upon our
littleness and in <u>tender</u> expansiveness makes room
for Himself. Had we thought Him an intruder?
Nay, God's first odor is sweetness, God's touch an
imparting of power. Suddenly, a tender giant walks
by our side, no, strides within our puny footsteps.
We are no longer our little selves. As two bodies
closely fastened together and whirled in the air
revolve in part about the heavier body, so life gets a
new center, from which we *are moved*. It is as if the
center of life had been shifted beyond ourselves, so
that we are no longer our old selves. Paul speaks
truly when he says that <u>we no longer live, but Christ</u>
<u>lives in us</u>, dynamic, energetic, creative, persuasive.
In hushed amazement at this majestic Other, our little
self grows still and listens for whispers—oh some so
faint—and yields itself like a little child to its true
Father-guidance. Yes, the sheep surely knows its

shepherd, in these holy moments of eternity.

The old self, the little self—how weak it is, and how absurdly confident and how absurdly timid it has been! How jealously we guard its strange precious pride! Famished for superiority-feeling, as Alfred Adler pointed out, its defeats must be offset by a dole of petty victories. In religious matters we still thought that we should struggle to present to God a suitable offering of service. We planned, we prayed, we suffered, we carried the burden. The we, the self, how subtly it intrudes itself into religion! And then steals in, so sweetly, so all-replacing, the sense of Presence, the sense of Other; and He plans, and He bears the burdens; and we are a new creature. Prayer becomes not hysterical cries to a distant God, but gentle upliftings and faint whispers, in which it is not easy to say *who* is speaking, we, or an Other through us. Perhaps we can only say: Praying is taking place. Power *flows* through us, from the Eternal into the rivulets of Time. Amazed, yet *not* amazed, we stride the stride of the tender giant who dwells within us, and wonders are performed. Active as never before, one lives in the passive voice, alert to be used, fearful of nothing, patient to stand and wait.

It is an amazing discovery, at first, to find that a creative power and Life is at work in the world. God is no longer the object of a belief; He is a Reality, who has continued, within us, His real Presence in the world. God is aggressive. He is an intruder, a lofty lowly conqueror on whom we had counted too little, because we had counted on ourselves. Too long have we supposed that we must carry the banner of religion, that it was *our* concern. But religion is not our concern; it is God's concern. Our task is to call people to "be still, and know that I am God," to hearken to that of God within them, to invite, to unclasp the clenched fists of self-resolution, to be pliant in His firm guidance, sensitive to the inflections of the inner voice.

For there is a life beyond earnestness to be found. It is the life rooted and grounded in the Presence, the Life which has *been found* by the Almighty. Seek it, seek it. Yet it lies beyond seeking. It arises in *being found*. To have come only as far as religious determination is only to have stood in the vestibule. But our confidence in our shrewdness, in our education, in our talents, in some aspect or other of our self-assured self, is our own undoing. So earnestly busy with anxious, fevered efforts for the Kingdom of God have we been, that we failed to hear the knock upon the door, and to know that our chief task is to open that door and be entered by the Divine Life.

ꚍHE NAꚍURE OF HOLY OBEDIENCE

From "Holy Obedience" in *A Testament of Devotion*

In March of 1939, Kelly delivered the William Penn Lecture to the Yearly Meeting of Quakers in the United States. It was printed as "Holy Obedience" and circulated widely. In this selection, Kelly talks about what it means to be completely obedient to God.

Meister Eckhart wrote: "There are plenty to follow our Lord half-way, but not the other half. They will give up possessions, friends and honors, but it touches them too closely to disown themselves." It is just this astonishing life which is willing to follow God the other half, sincerely to disown itself, this life which intends *complete* obedience, without *any* reservations, that I would propose to you in all humility, in all boldness, in all seriousness. I mean this literally, utterly, completely, and I mean it for you and for me—commit your lives in unreserved obedience to Him.

If you don't realize the revolutionary explosiveness of this proposal you don't understand what I mean. Only now and then comes a man or a woman who, like John Woolman or Francis of Assisi, is willing to be utterly obedient, to go the other half, to follow God's faintest whisper. But when such a commitment comes in a human life, God breaks through, miracles are wrought, world-renewing divine forces are released, history changes. There is nothing more important now than to have the human race endowed with just such committed lives. Now is no time to say, "Lo, here. Lo, there." Now is the time to say, "Thou art the man." To this extraordinary life I call you — or He calls you through me — not as a lovely ideal, a charming pattern to aim at hopefully, but as a serious, concrete program of life, to be lived here and now, in industrial America, by you and by me.

This is something wholly different from mild, conventional religion which, with respectable skirts held back by dainty fingers, anxiously tries to fish the world out of the mudhole of its own selfishness. Our churches, our meeting houses are full of such respectable and amiable people. We have plenty of Quakers to follow God the first half of the way. Many of us have become as mildly and as conventionally religious as were the church folk of three centuries ago, against whose mildness and mediocrity and passionlessness George Fox and his followers flung themselves with all the passion of a glorious and a new discovery and with all the energy of dedicated lives. In some, says William James, religion exists as a dull habit, in others as an acute fever. Religion as a dull habit is not that for which Christ lived and died.

There is a degree of holy and complete obedience and of joyful self-renunciation and of sensitive listening that is breathtaking. Difference of degree passes over into utter difference of kind, when one tries to follow Him the second half. Jesus put this pointedly when He said, "[Ye must] be born again" (John 3:3), and Paul knew it: "If any man be in Christ, he is a new creature" (2 Cor. 5:17).

George Fox as a youth was religious enough to meet all earthly standards and was even proposed as a student for the ministry. But the insatiable God-hunger in him drove him from such mediocrity into a passionate quest for the real whole-wheat Bread of Life. Sensible relatives told him to settle down and get married. Thinking him crazy, they took him to a doctor to have his blood let—the equivalent of being taken to a psychiatrist in these days, as are modern conscientious objectors to war in Belgium and France. Parents, if some of your children are seized with this imperative God-hunger, don't tell them to snap out of it and get a job, but carry them patiently in your love, or at least keep hands off and let the holy work of God proceed in their souls. Young people, you who have in you the stirrings of perfection, the sweet, sweet rapture of God Himself within you, be faithful to Him until the last lingering bit of self is surrendered and you are wholly God-possessed.

The life that intends to be wholly obedient, wholly submissive, wholly listening, is astonishing in its completeness. Its joys are ravishing, its peace profound, its humility the deepest, its power world-shaking, its love enveloping, its simplicity that of a trusting child. It is the life and power in which the prophets and apostles lived. It is the life and power of Jesus of Nazareth, who knew that "when thine eye is single, thy whole body is full of light" (Luke

11:34). It is the life and power of the apostle Paul, who resolved not to know anything among men save Jesus Christ and Him crucified. It is the life and power of Saint Francis, that little poor man of God who came nearer to re-living the life of Jesus than has any other man on earth. It is the life and power of George Fox and of Isaac and Mary Penington. It is the life and power and utter obedience of John Woolman who decided, he says, "to place my whole trust in God," to "act on an inner Principle of Virtue, and pursue worldly business no farther than as Truth opened my way therein." It is the life and power of myriads of unknown saints through the ages. It is the life and power of some people now in this room who smile knowingly as I speak. And it is a life and power that can break forth in this tottering Western culture and return the church to its rightful life as a fellowship of creative, heaven-led souls.

◫ GATEWAYS INTO HOLY OBEDIENCE

From "Holy Obedience" in *A Testament of Devotion*

Here Kelly speaks of the steps by which one may grow in obedience to God.

1   The first step to the obedience of the second half is the flaming vision of the wonder of such a life, a vision which comes occasionally to us all, through biographies of the saints, through the journals of Fox and early Friends, through a life lived before our eyes, through a haunting verse of the Psalms — "Whom have I in heaven but Thee? And there is none upon earth that I desire besides Thee" (Ps. 73:25) — through meditation upon the amazing life and death of Jesus, through a flash of illumination or, in Fox's language, a great opening. But whatever the earthly history of this moment of charm, this vision of an absolutely holy life is, I am convinced, the invading, urging, inviting, persuading work of the Eternal One. It is curious that modern psychology cannot account wholly for flashes of insight of any kind, sacred or secular. It is as if a fountain of creative Mind were welling up, bubbling to expression within prepared spirits. There is an infinite fountain of lifting power, pressing within us, luring us by dazzling visions, and we can only say, The creative God comes into our souls. An increment of infinity is about us. Holy is imagination, the gateway of Reality

into our hearts. The Hound of Heaven is on our track, the God of Love is wooing us to His Holy Life.

Once having the vision, the second step to holy obedience is this: Begin where you are. Obey *now*. Use what little obedience you are capable of, even if it be like a grain of mustard seed. Begin where you are. Live this present moment, this present hour as you now sit in your seats, in utter, utter submission and openness toward Him. Listen outwardly to these words, but within, behind the scenes, in the deeper levels of your lives where you are all alone with God the Loving Eternal One, keep up a silent prayer, "Open Thou my life. Guide my thoughts where I dare not let them go. But Thou darest. Thy will be done." Walk on the streets and chat with your friends. But every moment behind the scenes be in prayer, offering yourselves in continuous obedience. I find this internal continuous prayer life absolutely essential. It can be carried on day and night, in the thick of business, in home and school. Such prayer of submission can be so simple. It is well to use a single sentence, repeated over and over and over again, such as this: "Be Thou my will. Be Thou my will," or "I open all before Thee. I open all before Thee," or "See earth through heaven. See earth through heaven." This hidden prayer life can pass, in time, beyond words and phrases into mere ejaculations, "My God, my God, my Holy One, my Love," or into the adoration of the Upanishad, "O Wonderful, O Wonderful, O Wonderful." Words may cease and one stands and walks and sits and lies in wordless attitudes of adoration and submission and rejoicing and exultation and glory.

3   And the third step in holy obedience, or a counsel, is this: If you slip and stumble and forget God for an hour, and assert your old proud self, and rely upon your own clever wisdom, don't spend too much time in anguished regrets and self-accusations but begin again, just where you are.

4   Yet a fourth consideration in holy obedience is this: Don't grit your teeth and clench your fists and say, "I will! I will!" Relax. Take hands off. Submit yourself to God. Learn to live in the passive voice—a hard saying for Americans—and let life be willed through you. For "I will" spells not obedience.

INSIGHTS FROM GEORGE FOX

From "The Quaker Discovery" in *The Eternal Promise*

This essay was printed in The Friend, *a Quaker maga-zine, in December 1939. Kelly reflects on the life of George Fox, the founder of the Society of Friends. Fox had searched for someone who would help him to find and know God, help him to rise above the mediocre, lukewarm religion he saw around him. He tried many guides, clergy and lay, but was repeatedly disappointed.*

Thus he was driven from all outer aids, and was forced back *within* himself for *inner* insights and guidance. The very first constructive insight, the first inward ray of light which he reports, has to do with the *whole of Christendom*, the entire Christian Church. "About the beginning of 1646, as I was going to Coventry, and entering towards the gates, a consider-ation arose in me, how it was said that all Christians are believers, both Protestants and Papists; and the Lord opened to me that, if all were believers, then they were all born of God, and passed from death to life, and that none were true believers but such; and though others said they were believers, yet were they not."

This was not a narrowing of the gate of Truth. Fox had no thought of or interest in founding a little sect which should play upon a single string and call its music the whole of truth. *All* are in the life of God, whether Protestant or Catholic, who have been "born of God," who have been brought into God's immediate fellowship, who have become children of God (for whom, as Paul says, the whole creation groaneth and travaileth in pain, until such be born). And none who have never been brought into God's immediacy are even Christians at all, no matter if they are members of a church and have the best gilt-edged credentials of an outward sort. Religion is in nothing outward; no church can save us. Religion is *inward*, it arises in immediacy of relation with God. It involves new blood in our veins. It involves the life-blood of each of us, so that we can say, "My Father. I am in His family. I have fellowship in His love."

Another dawning insight which broke in upon him was that there is no substitute for *immediacy of revelation*. Each individual soul must and can have direct illumination inside himself, from the living, revealing Spirit of God, now, today, for He is active in the world. The form of this dawning insight in Fox had to do with what fitted a person to be a minister. He says, "At another time, as I was walking in a field on a First Day morning, the Lord opened to me that being bred at Oxford or Cambridge was not enough to fit and qualify men to be ministers of Christ." That is to say, in modern terms: You can go to theological seminary, and study *about* religion. You can learn the history of the Christian Church. You can know all about the Synoptic problems of the Gospels and have your own theories about Q and the J, E, D, and P documents of the Hexateuch; you can know all the literature about the authorship of the Johannine epistles, whether the author was John the beloved disciple or another of the same name. You can know all about the history of Quakerism; you can know the disputes behind the Nicene Creed and the Constantinopolitan Creed. You can know the Westminster Confession and the Augsburg Confession and the Thirty-nine Articles of the Church of England. You can know homiletics and rules of good sermon structure. You can know church symbolism and the meaning of the feasts and fasts of the church. You can know all this, and much more. But unless you _know God_, immediately, every day communing with Him, rejoicing in Him, exalting in Him, opening your life in joyful obedience toward Him and feeling Him speaking to you and guiding you into ever fuller loving obedience to Him, you aren't fit to be a minister. There is so much that is wonderful in books. But he who relies for his sermons upon book-stuff _about_ religion, and is not at the same time enjoying immediately and experiencing vitally fresh illumination from God, is not a real minister, even if he has a degree in theology from Oxford or Cambridge. Secondhand sermons aren't _real_ sermons. Only firsthand preaching counts. He is a minister who is given a message within himself, as a fresh insight from God, transmitted _through him_ to others.

Another insight which came to him had to do with churches and temples. The church building is not a church, the brick and mortar structure is not a church. God doesn't live in a house with a peaked roof. God lives inside people. And if God isn't inside you, you needn't expect to find him in a house with a peaked roof that is outside you. God is within. And where He dwells, there is a holy place. Fox was finding he had an altar inside his own soul. Inside him was a hushed and holy Presence, too sacred to be destroyed, too wonderful not to be visited continually. The holy Presence was Inward. Fox found Him there, and all life was new. It is a wonderful discovery, to find that you are a temple, that you have a church *inside* you, where God is. There is something awful, that is, awe-inspiring, down at the depths of our own soul. In hushed silence attend to it. It is a whisper of God Himself, particularizing Himself for you and in you, and speaking to the world through you. God isn't dead. "The Lord is in his holy temple; let all the earth keep silence before him."

All of these insights are such as wean us away from confusing religious information with external things, with external church membership, with external church doctrines, external church habitations. In place of these, Fox went inward, and there found resplendent glory of God's immediacy and love and power and guidance and sufficiency. And this is a true insight, which finds the inner sanctuary of the soul to be the Home of God. As long as outwards are counted as essential, we are no better than those reported by the Samaritan woman to Jesus: "Shall we worship in this mountain or in Jerusalem?" Shall we perform this ceremony or that? Shall we assent to this statement or a different one? Christianity needs to get behind its still lingering confusion about the essential character of *any* external, even as beautiful as that of dramatizing the Lord's Supper with His disciples, and put first of all the sacrament of the heart, where God and human break bread together in the secret sanctuary of the soul.

PRACTICING THE PRESENCE OF GOD

From *Reality of the Spiritual World*

In December 1940 and January 1941, Kelly gave a series of four lectures on the spiritual life at Pendle Hill, a Quaker center for exploration and education near Philadelphia. He gave the final talk just a few days before his death. The talks were published as a Pendle Hill Pamphlet in 1942. In this selection, Kelly talks about how we can begin to pray without ceasing.

This practice of continuous prayer in the presence of God involves developing the habit of carrying on the mental life at two levels. At one level we are immersed in this world of time, of daily affairs. At the same time, but at a deeper level of our minds, we are in active relation with the Eternal Life. I do not think this is a psychological impossibility, or an abnormal thing. One sees a mild analogy in the very human experience of being in love. The newly accepted lover has an internal life of joy, of bounding heart, of outgoing aspiration toward his beloved. Yet he goes to work, earns his living, eats his meals, pays his bills. But all the time deep within, there is a level of awareness of an object very dear to him. This awareness is private; he shows it to no one; yet it spills across and changes his outer life, colors his behavior, and gives new zest and glory to the daily round. Oh yes, we know what a mooning calf he may be at first, what a lovable fool about outward affairs. But when the lover gets things in focus again, and husband and wife settle down to the long pull of the years, the deep love-relation underlies all the raveling frictions of home life, and recreates them in the light of the deeper currents of love. The two levels are there, the surface and the deeper, in fruitful interplay with the creative values coming from the deeper into the daily affairs of life.

So it is sometimes when one becomes a lover of God. One's first experience of the Heavenly Splendor plows through one's whole being, makes one dance and sing inwardly, enthralls one in unspeakable love. Then the world, at first, is all out of focus; we scorn it, we are abstracted, we are drunken with Eternity. We have not yet learned how to live in both worlds at once, how to integrate our life in time fruitfully with Eternity. Yet we are beings whose home is both here and Yonder, and we must learn the secret of being at home in both, all the time. A new level of our being has been opened to us, and lo, it is Immanuel, God with us. The experience of the Presence of God is not something plastered on to our nature; it is the fulfillment of ourselves. The last deeps of humanity go down into the life of God. The stabilizing of our lives, so that we live in God and in time, in fruitful interplay, is the task of maturing religious life.

How do you begin this double mental life, this life at two levels? You begin *now*, wherever you are. Listen to these words outwardly. But, within, deep within you, continue in steady prayer, offering yourself and all that you are to Him in simple, joyful, serene, unstrained dedication. Practice it steadily. Make it your conscious intention. Keep it up for days and weeks and years. You will be swept away by rapt attention to the exciting things going on around you. Then catch yourself and bring yourself back. You will forget God for whole hours. But do not waste any time in bitter regrets or self-recriminations. Just begin again. The first weeks and months of such practice are pretty patchy, badly botched. But say inwardly to yourself and to God, "This is the kind of bungling person I am when I am not wholly Thine. But take this imperfect devotion of these months and transmute it with Thy love."

Then begin again. And gradually, in months or in three or four years, the habit of heavenly orientation becomes easier, more established. The times of your wandering become shorter, less frequent. The stability of your deeper level becomes greater; God becomes a more steady background of all your reactions in the time-world. Down in this center you have a Holy Place, a *Shekinah*, where you and God hold sweet converse. Your outer behavior will be revised and your personal angularities will be melted down, and you will approach the outer world of people with something more like an outgoing divine love, directed toward them. You begin to love others, because you live in love toward God. Or the divine love flows out toward others through you and you become His pliant instrument of loving concern.

FIVE VARIETIES OF PRAYER

From *Reality of the Spiritual World*

Here Kelly discusses some of the forms that interior prayer may take.

First, there is what I can only call the *prayer of oblation,* the prayer of pouring yourself out before God. You pray inwardly, "Take all of me, take all of me." Back behind the scenes of daily occupation you offer yourself steadily to God, you pour out all your life and will and love before Him, and try to keep nothing back. Pour out your triumphs before Him. But pour out also the rags and tatters of your mistakes before Him. If you make a slip and get angry, pour out that bit of anger before Him and say, "That too is Thine." If an evil thought flashes through your mind, pour that out before Him and say, "I know that looks pretty shabby, when it is brought into the sanctuary of Thy holiness. But that's what I am, except Thou aidest me."

When you meet a friend, outwardly you chat with him about trivial things. But inwardly offer him to God. Say within yourself, "Here is my friend. Break in upon him. Melt him down. Help him to shake off the scales from his eyes and see Thee. Take him."

Shall I go on and say how far I would carry the prayer of oblation? Some cases may sound strange and silly. Do you stumble on a cinder? Offer it to God, as a part of the world that belongs to Him. Do you pass a tree? That too is His; give it to Him as His own. Do you read the newspaper and see the vast panorama of humanity struggling in blindness, in selfish deficient living? Offer humanity, in all its shabbiness and in all its grandeur, and hold it up into the heart of Love within you.

At first you make these prayers in words, in little sentences, and say them over and over again. "Here is my life, here is my life." In the morning you say, "This is Thy day, this is Thy day." In the evening you say of the day, "Receive it. Accept it. It is Thine." But in the course of the months you find yourself passing beyond words, and merely living in attitudes of oblation to which the words used to give expression. A gesture of the soul toward God is a prayer; a more or less steady lifting of everything you touch, a lifting of it high before Him, to be transmuted in His love. If you grow careless in such unworded gestures and attitudes, you can always return to the practice of worded prayers of oblation, to fix your inner attention and retrain your habit of prayer. "Thou wilt keep him in perfect peace whose mind is stayed on thee."

Then there is the *prayer of inward song.* Phrases run through the background of your mind. "Bless the Lord, O my soul; and all that is within me, bless his holy name." "My soul doth magnify the Lord, and my spirit hath rejoiced in God my Savior." Inner exultation, inner glorification of the wonders of God fill the deeper level of mind. Sometimes this is a background of deep-running joy and peace; sometimes it is a dancing, singing torrent of happiness, which you must take measures to hide from the world lest people think you are like the apostles at Pentecost, filled with new wine. Pentecost ought to be here; it can be here, in this very place, in wartime. Christians who don't know an inner pentecostal joy are living contradictions of Christianity. Outward sobriety is dictated by a fine sense of the fittingness of things. But inward fires should burn in the God-kindled soul, fires shining outward in a radiant and released personality. Inwardly, there are hours of joy in God, and the songs of the soul are ever rising. Sometimes the singer and the song seem to be merged together as a single offering to the God of Joy. Sometimes He who puts the new song into our mouths seems merged with the song and the singer, and it is not we alone who sing, but the Eternal Lover who sings through us and out into the world where songs have died on many lips.

In such moods I find the Book of Psalms wonderfully helpful. There we come into contact with souls who have risen above debate and argument and problem-discussion, and have become singers of the Song of Eternal Love. We read the Psalms hungrily. They say in words what we try to express. Our private joy in God becomes changed into a fellowship of singing souls. The writers of the Psalms teach us new songs of the heart. They give us great phrases that go rolling through our minds all the day long.

They channel our prayer of song. Religious reading ought not to be confined to heady, brainy, argumentative discussion, important as that is. Every profoundly religious soul ought to rise to the level of inward psalm-singing; he ought to read devotional literature that is psalm-like in character and spirit. The little book of prayers, *A Chain of Prayers across the Ages*, is excellent. And Thomas à Kempis's *Imitation of Christ* often gives voice to the song of the soul.

Then there is the *prayer of inward listening*. Perhaps this is not a separate type of prayer, but an element that interlaces the whole of the internal prayer-life. For prayer is a two-way process. It is not just human souls whispering to God. It passes over into communion, with God active in us, as well as we active toward God. A specific state of expectancy, of openness of soul is laid bare and receptive before the Eternal Goodness. In quietness we wait, inwardly, in unformulated expectation. Perhaps this is best done in retirement. Our church services ought to be times when bands of expectant souls gather and wait before Him. But too often, for myself, the external show of the ritual keeps my expectations chained to earth, to this room, to see what the choir will sing, to hear how the minister handles the theme. Much of Protestant worship seems to me to keep expectation at the earthly level of watchfulness for helpful external stimuli, external words, external suggestions. Perhaps because I am a Quaker I find the prayer of expectation and of listening easiest to carry on in the silence of solitary and of group meditation.

Creative, Spirit-filled lives do not arise until God is attended to, till His internal teaching, in warm immediacy, becomes a real experience. He has many things to say to us, but we cannot hear Him now, because we have not been wholly weaned away from outward helps, valuable as these often are. The living Christ teaches the listening soul, and guides him into new truth. Sad is it if our church program is so filled with noise, even beautiful sound, that it distracts us from the listening life, the expectation directed toward God. A living silence is often more creative, more recreative, than verbalized prayers worded in gracious phrases.

We need also times of silent waiting, alone, when the busy intellect is not leaping from problem to problem, and from puzzle to puzzle. If we learn the secret of carrying a living silence in the center of our being we can listen on the run. The listening silence can become intertwined with all our inward prayers. A few moments of relaxed silence, alone, every day, are desperately important. When distracting noises come, don't fight against them, do not elbow them out, but accept them and weave them by prayer into the silence. Does the wind rattle the window? Then pray, "So let the wind of the Spirit shake the Christian church into life," and absorb it into the silent listening. Does a child cry in the street outside? Then pray, "So cries my infant soul, which does not know the breadth of Thy heart," and absorb it into the silent listening prayer.

The last reaches of religious education are not

attained by carefully planned and externally applied lessons, taught to people through the outward ears. The fundamental religious education of the soul is conducted by the Holy Spirit, the living voice of God within us. He is the last and greatest teacher of the soul. All else are but pointings to the inward Teacher, the Spirit of the indwelling Christ. Until life is lived in the presence of this Teacher, we are apt to confuse knowledge of church history and biblical backgrounds with the true education of the soul that takes place in the listening life of prayer.

A fourth form of inner prayer is what I call the *prayer of carrying*. This I shall not try to develop now, but shall discuss later in connection with the experience of group fellowship among those who are deep in the life and love of God. But it consists essentially in a well-nigh continuous support, in prayer, of some particular souls who are near to you in the things of the inner life.

I must, however, speak more at length of a fifth aspect of internal prayer. The Catholic books call it *infused prayer*. There come times, to some people at least, when one's prayer is given to one, as it were from beyond oneself. Most of the time we ourselves seem to pick the theme of our prayer. We seem to be the conscious initiators. We decide what prayers we shall lift before the Throne. But there come amazing times, in the practice of prayer, when our theme of prayer is laid upon us, as if initiated by God Himself. This is an astonishing experience. It is as if we were being prayed through by a living Spirit. How can it be that the indwelling Christ prompts us to breathe back to God a prayer that originates in Himself? Is there a giant circle of prayer, such that prayer may originate in God and swing down into us and back up unto Himself? I can only say that it seems to be that way. And it seems to be an instance of the giant circle in religious dedication, whereby we seek because we have already been found by Him. Our seeking is already His finding. Our return to the Father is but the completion of His going out to us.

In the experience of infused prayer there seems to be some blurring of the distinctions between the one who prays, the prayer that is prayed, and the One to whom the prayer is prayed. Do we pray, or does God pray through us? I know not. All I can say is, prayer is taking place, and we are graciously permitted to be within the orbit. We emerge from such experiences of infused prayer shaken and deepened and humbled before the Majesty on High. And we somehow know that we have been given some glimpse of that Life, that Center of Wonder, before Whom every knee should bow and every tongue that knows the language of its Homeland should confess the adorable mercy of God.

NEW FELLOWSHIP

From *Reality of the Spiritual World*

In his final Pendle Hill lecture, Kelly talks about the new fellowship one discovers with others who know God's abiding presence.

When our souls are utterly swept through and overturned by God's invading love, we suddenly find ourselves in the midst of a wholly new relationship with some of our fellow human beings. We find ourselves enmeshed with some people in amazing bonds of love and nearness and togetherness of soul, such as we never knew before. In glad amazement we ask ourselves: What is this startling new bondedness in love which I feel with those who are down in the same center of life? Can this amazing experience of togetherness in love be what people have called fellowship? Can this be the love which bound together the early church, and made their meals together into a sacrament of love? Is this internal impulse which I feel, to share life with those who are down in the same center of love, the reason that the Early Church members shared their outward goods as a symbol of the experienced internal sharing of the life and the love of Christ? Can this new bondedness in love be the meaning of being in the kingdom of God?

But not all our acquaintances are caught with these new and special bonds of love. A rearrangement takes place. Some people whom we had only slightly known before suddenly become electrically illuminated. Now we know them, for lo, they have been down in the center a long time, and we never knew their secret before. Now we are bound together with them in a special bond of nearness, far exceeding the nearness we feel toward many we have known for years. For we know where they live, and they know where we live, and we understand one another and are powerfully drawn to one another. We hunger for their fellowship; their lives are knitted with our life in this amazing bondedness of divine love.

Others of our acquaintance recede in importance. We may have known them for years; we may have thought we were close together. But now we know they are not down in the center in Christ, where our dearest loves and hopes of life and death are focused. And we know we can never share life at its depth until they, too, find their way down into this burning center of shared love.

Especially does a new alignment of our church relationship take place. Now we know, from within, the secret of the perseverance and fidelity of some, a secret we could not have guessed when we were *outside* them. *Now* we see, suddenly, that some of the active leaders are not so far down into the center of peace and love as we had supposed. We had always respected and admired them for their energy, but now we know they have never been brought into the depths, nor do they know the secret of being rooted and grounded with others in love. Now we suddenly see that some quiet, obscure persons, whose voices count for little in the councils of the church, are princes and saints in Israel. Why had we not noticed them before? The whole graded scale by which we had arranged the people in our church according to importance is shaken and revised. Some of the leaders are greater even than we had guessed; others are thin and anxious souls, not knowing the peace at the center. Some that stood low are really high in the new range of values.

Into this fellowship of souls at the center we simply emerge. No one is chosen to the fellowship. When we discover God we discover the fellowship. When we find ourselves in Christ we find we are also amazingly united with those others who are also in Christ. When we were outside of it we never knew that it existed or only dimly guessed the existence of bonds of love among those who were dedicated slaves of Christ. There are many who are members of our churches who do not know what I am speaking of. But there are others of you who will say, "Surely I know exactly what you are talking about. I'm glad you've found your way in."

OPENING TO THE WORLD

From "Excerpts from The Richard Cary Lecture"
in *The Eternal Promise*

As we grow open to God (the subject of the beginning of the lecture), we also grow open to the world around us. Kelly turns to this subject near the end of the lecture.

Formerly the world spread itself out before us, focused about ourselves. We were the center. All our enjoyment, of things and people, was for us, to exploit, to rearrange, to clamber over, to conquer. The effective limits of our world were the limits of its utility or importance for us. The world-managing attitude has reigned with peculiar force in modern times. And in this attitude, taken in solitary predominance, lie all the seeds of war. And in this world-managing epoch we all, as individuals and as nations, carry over into our working hours the fantasy-life of the daydreams, with its center in the conquering hero or the suffering hero. In this respect, the modern person tends to be far indeed from that spirit which is near to the center of religion, the final joyful submission of all one's being to the Holy, the feeling of absolute dependence of Schleiermacher.

But in the Eternal Presence, the world spreads itself out, not as our little world, but as the world of God. And we sigh; at last we awake. And now we must say — it sounds blasphemous, but mystics are repeatedly charged with blasphemy—now we must say it is given to us to see the world's suffering, *throughout*, and bear it, Godlike, upon our shoulders, and suffer with all things and all people, and rejoice with all things and all people, and we see the hills clap their hands for joy, and we clap our hands with them. A friend has told me how it was given to her to see the entirety of the evil of the world, on its back-side, so to say, and to look *through* it, into the face of God. That I have not seen. But suffering and the joy and the serenity at the heart of the world—these are unspeakably great. Were one not assisted, one could not bear it. It is an awful thing to fall into the hands of the living God. It was truly said by George Fox, "I was come up through the flaming sword into the paradise of God." But there is a point of vision from which one can look through sorrow and pain and still see the face of the Eternal Lover. This is a hard saying, but worthy of all acceptation.

It is frequently said that to bear this world, we must become toughened, callous, hard. The sadness of the city-evils, the blighted lives we see, the injustices, the pain and tears! Without a protective covering of indifference, it seems rational to say we cannot endure the world. But the Eternal Presence, shining upon time, gives us, not a tough protection, but an exquisitely *tendered* spirit. Overburdened men and women, blighted lives, slaveries in all their modern forms, nations and institutions in insane self-destruction, and little children hoping for warmth and love and opportunity [are all laid upon us]. To our easier sympathy with physical pain there is added suffering because of the soul-blindness which we see everywhere. To see hatred poison a life is suffering indeed. The self-seeking, so-called "successful person," who has missed the holy way, is as saddening as the drunkard or the criminal. In the figure of John Bunyan one says: Why do people rake together the sticks and straws of the world, when their heads are offered the crown of life! Before, our chief suffering, the suffering about which we are disturbed, was *our own* suffering. The world's arrows were thought to be aimed at us. But with the great unselfing, the center of concern for suffering is shifted *outside* ourselves and distributed with breadth unbounded among all, friends and so-called enemies. For a few agonized moments we may seem to be given to stand *within* the heart of the World-Father and feel the infinite sufferings of love toward all the Father's children. And pain inflicted on them becomes pain inflicted on ourselves. Were the experience not also an experience suffused with radiant peace and power and victory, as well as tragedy, it would be unbearable.

SEEDS OF AWARENESS, SPRINGS OF HOPE

From "Where Are the Springs of Hope?"
in *The Eternal Promise*

The occasion for this talk is unknown. It was printed in Motive *after Kelly's death. Kelly is reflecting on a phrase from Psalm 126: "They that go forth in tears, bearing their seed with them, shall return in joy" (author's translation).*

The important thing here is the phrase, *bearing their seed with them.* Only those who go forth in tears, and who bear with them into their suffering some awakened seed, shall return in hope.

There is nothing automatic about suffering, so that suffering infallibly produces great souls. We have passed out of the prewar days when we believed in the escalator theory of progress. Those were the boom days of economic and churchly prosperity, when we thought that every day in every way we were growing better and better and we thought that the kingdom of God on earth was just around the corner, if we, in *laissez faire* style, cooperated and didn't halt the process. Then it seemed easy to speak words of hope and to prod the last laggards into feverish activity to run the last mile of the race to the millennium. But now in the light of world war we are forced to abandon that easy view and go infinitely deeper. Now that suffering is upon the world we cannot appeal to the escalator theory of suffering and expect that suffering will inevitably shake great souls into life. No, there is nothing about suffering such that it automatically purges the dross from human nature and brings heroic souls upon the scene. Suffering can blast and blight an earnest but unprepared soul, and damn it utterly to despair.

No, only those who go into the travail of today, *bearing a seed within them*, a seed of awareness of the heavenly dimensions of humanity, can return in joy. Where this seed of divine awareness is quickened and grows, there Calvary is enacted again in joy. And Calvary is still the hope of the world. Each one of us has the seed of Christ within. In each of us the amazing and the dangerous seed of Christ is present. It is only a seed. It is very small, like the grain of mustard seed. The Christ that is formed in us is small indeed, but He is great with eternity. But if we dare to take this awakened seed of Christ into the midst of the world's suffering, it will grow. That's why the Quaker work camps are important. Take a young man or young woman in whom Christ is only dimly formed, but one in whom the seed of Christ is alive. Put him into a distressed area, into a refugee camp, into a poverty region. Let him go into the world's suffering, bearing this seed with him, and in suffering it will *grow*, and Christ will be more and more fully formed in him. As the grain of mustard seed grew so large that the birds found shelter in it, so the one who bears an awakened seed into the world's suffering will grow until he becomes a refuge for many.

This is one of the springs of hope—the certainty that the seed of Christ is in us all (Quakers have also called it the inner light) and the confidence that many of those who call themselves Christian will enter suffering, bearing this seed with them, *daring* to let it germinate, *daring* to let it take them through personal risk and financial loss and economic insecurity, up the steep slopes of some obscure Calvary. Ponder this carefully: Our right to life, liberty, and the pursuit of happiness is not absolute. We dare not claim them as our absolute right. For the seed of Christ that we bear into the world's suffering will teach us to renounce these as our own, and strip us, in utter poverty of soul and perhaps of body, until our only hope is in the eternal goodness of God.

In you is this seed. Do you not feel its quickening Life? Then, small though this seed be in you, sow your life into the furrows of the world's suffering, and you will return in joy, and the world will arise in hope. For Christ is born again, and is dying again on Calvary and rising victorious from the tomb.

The second spring of hope is this: We simple, humble people can bear the seed of hope. No religious dictator will save the world; no giant figure of heroic size will stalk across the stage of history today, as a new Messiah. But in simple, humble, imperfect people like you and me wells up the spring of hope. We have this treasure of the seed in earthen vessels — very earthen vessels. You and I know how imperfect we are. And yet those little demonstrations of love and goodwill, such as the feeding of children in

Spain, the direction of transit stations for refugees in Holland and Cuba, the reconstruction of lives in the coal fields, are being carried on by just such earthen vessels. These tasks shine like tiny candles in the darkness—deeds done in the midst of suffering, through which shines the light of the Living Christ, deeds that stir hope that humanity as a whole will be aroused to yield to the press and surge of the Eternal Love within them. For the Eternal Love is beating in upon us, upon you and upon me, quickening the seed within us into life. Our very weakness, as humans, is the fit soil for divine awakening. If you are proud and self-confident and sure you are no earthen vessel, then the greatness of the divine fructifying power will never be awakened in you. Yield yourselves to the growth of the seed within you, in these our days of suffering. Sow yourselves into the furrows of the world's pain, and hope will grow and rise high. Be not overcome by the imposing forces of evil and of might. Be of good cheer, says Jesus, *I have overcome the world.* But there is no hope if Calvary is only an external Calvary. Within you must the Living Christ be formed, until you are led within yourselves to die wholly that you may wholly live. Then will Christ again walk the ways of the world's sorrows. In Him alone, and in you so far as Christ is formed in you, is the hope of the world. There is no cheaper hope than Calvary, no panacea other than awakened love that leads us into the world's suffering into victory.

special
concerns

This article was published in early summer of 1938, just before Kelly left for Germany. It formed the basis for The Richard Cary Lecture, which he gave there. Here, Kelly speaks about what Quakers call "concerns"—particular issues for which one feels called to a special responsibility.

There are two ways in which a concern is a particularization. It is a particularization of the Divine Concern of God for all creation. God's love isn't just a diffused benevolence. As the Eternal is the root and ground of all times, yet breaks into particular moments, so the Infinite Love is the ground of all creatures, the source of their existence, and also knows a tender concern for each, and guides those who are sensitive to this tender care into a mutually supporting Blessed Fraternity.

But it is a particularization of *my* responsibility also, in a world too vast and a lifetime too short for me to carry all responsibilities. My cosmic love, or the Divine Lover loving within me, cannot accomplish its full intent, *which is universal saviorhood*, within the limits of three score years and ten. But the Loving Presence does not burden us equally with all things, but considerately puts upon each of us just a few central tasks, as emphatic responsibilities. For each of us these special undertakings are our share in the joyous burdens of love.

Thus the state of having a concern has a foreground and a background. In the foreground is the special task, uniquely illuminated, toward which we feel a special yearning and care. This is the concern as we usually talk about it or present it to the Monthly Meeting. But in the background is a second level, or layer, of universal concern for all the multitude of good things that need doing. Toward them all we feel kindly, but we are dismissed from active service in most of them. And we have an easy mind in the presence of desperately real needs which are not our direct responsibility. We cannot die on *every* cross, nor are we expected to.

I wish I might emphasize how a life becomes simplified when dominated by faithfulness to a few concerns. Too many of us have too many irons in the fire. We get distracted by the intellectual claim to our interest in a thousand and one good things, and before we know it we are pulled and hauled breathlessly along by an overburdened program of good committees and good undertakings. I am persuaded that this fevered life of church workers is not wholesome. Undertakings get plastered on from the outside because we can't turn down a friend. Acceptance of service on a weighty committee should really depend upon an answering imperative within us, not merely upon a rational calculation of the factors involved. The concern-oriented life is ordered and organized from within. And we learn to say *No* as well

as *Yes* by attending to the guidance of inner responsibility. Quaker simplicity needs to be expressed not
merely in dress and architecture and the height of
tombstones but also in the structure of a relatively
simplified and coordinated life-program of social
responsibilities. And I am persuaded that *concerns*
introduce that simplification, and along with it that
intensification which we need in opposition to the
hurried, superficial tendencies of our age.

We have tried to discover the grounds of the
social responsibility and the social sensitivity of
Friends. It is not in mere humanitarianism. It is not
in mere pity. It is not in mere obedience to Bible
commands. It is not in anything earthly. The social
concern of Friends is grounded in an experience — an
experience of the Love of God and of the impulse to
saviorhood inherent in the fresh quickenings of that
Life. Social concern is the dynamic Life of God at
work in the world, made special and emphatic and
unique, particularized in each individual or group
who is sensitive and tender in the leading-strings of
love. A concern is God-initiated, often surprising,
always holy, for the Life of God is breaking through
into the world. Its execution is in peace and power
and astounding faith and joy, for in unhurried
serenity the Eternal is at work in the midst of time,
triumphantly bringing all things up unto Himself.

ROYAL BLINDNESS

From "Have You Ever Seen a Miracle?"
in *The Eternal Promise*

This talk was given to a group of United Church of Christ ministers in 1940. This selection is the final portion of that talk. Kelly speaks of complete self-surrender leading to a "royal blindness" in which all social distinctions are leveled and we become "wholly God-enthralled."

Self-surrender becomes complete when we accept *all* God's dealings with our souls as a gift of His grace and as token of His love. Does God show His face and make us to sit down in heavenly places in Christ Jesus? Then thank God and be quietly but unboundedly grateful for His favor. Does God withdraw His inner consolation? Then thank God for the discipline He thus lays upon us, that we may be weaned away from dependence upon the highs and lows of mental changes and learn *solely to cling to Him*, and learn to love God purely for His own sake, and not for His gifts.

For spiritual maturity is not tested by the frequency of our mystical moments of exaltation, but by the glad and calm serenity of will in Him which is ours when barrenness and dryness come upon us. The Dark Night of the soul is an advanced course in the curriculum of the school of the Holy Spirit. And happy is one who has fulfilled the earlier prerequisites to whom is now entrusted this discipline of pain.

But it is not alone that we are freed from the changing sunshine and shadow of spiritual dryness and spiritual elevation, as we seek down, deep, below both, into quiet, resting of will in the Eternal Goodness. We reach a wholly new evaluation of outward things, a new indifference to personal fortunes or to fame as obscurity sets in. I like to call this the *royal blindness*. We grow blind to the petty valuations of the world. We grow blind to the petty eminences we have sought. We grow blind to the obscurity which is our lot, and, in no resentment, joyfully live in Eternity *just where we are.* Oh, we've known intellectually all these things for years, and have probably preached them from our pulpits. But there is an experience of finding all things leveled in the God-blinded eye which is utterly different from an intellectual belief in the unimportance of fame. With what pity we now look upon men and women whose whole life and love seem to be set upon puny perishing tinsel! And with what shame we look upon our own wasted years of yearning to be somebody. For now we see these things as they are: round-about ways of pleasing *our own little selves*, of freeing our own little selves from mental disquiet. Oh, we persuaded ourselves that we wanted a more prominent church, so we could have a bigger field of service, and help bring in the Kingdom more effectively. But now we know it was because we like the flattery of having people whisper behind our backs as we go by, "There goes so-and-so, he's quite an important man." And we've chafed in our tiny unnoticed niches because of wounded self-pride, because secretly we believed we were a bigger person than we got credit for being. Self-love, self-pride, self-seeking, self-inflation that would cover up its own poverty by accumulating an array of glittering earth garments of doctor's degrees and titles and honors and successes! But oh, how sinuous and subtle is self-pride. The enemy of complete dedication! We preach clever sermons, and quote learned authors and hope people will notice how well-read we are. Do you recall that wise minister to whom a doting parishioner said, "O, Doctor Jones, that was a wonderful sermon you preached this morning"? "Yes," replied the minister, "the Devil whispered that same thing to me, just as I was sitting down." Recall the words of Saint Paul, "We preach not ourselves but Christ Jesus the Lord; and ourselves your servants for Jesus' sake."

But the royal blindness levels all this, to the degree that all our self is willed into the life and love of God, in utmost dedication. We can look past the riches of a rich man, right through the imposing front of artificial importance, and as Jesus did with the rich young man, love him for what he is, and yearn over him as a human, God-hungry, perhaps earth-blinded soul; yearn that he may be stricken with the royal blindedness of Eternity so that he too sees all people as leveled and himself as a humble child of God, and his wealth as a barrier or an opportunity or a trust. We can look past the learning of the learned, and pray that they be loosed from pride in their learning and be humbled and born again as little children. For of such, not of professors, is the kingdom of Heaven.

And, O hardest test of all put upon the royal blindedness, we can meet the poor and the lowly in such utter sincerity of friendship and concern that some of them at least will find where the roots of our lives go down, and will look upon us with level eye and say, "I too am hungry for God. I too have seen some of His glory." But what terrible sincerity it takes. Only the simple directness of Jesus and of Francis of Assisi can do it. I am distressed that I know so many nice people, and have so few real personal friends among the Blacks and the roustabouts and the hopelessly submerged men and women. We try to pull the strings of political and social changes so as to better their broad environment. And all this is important. But Christ is not born in us until we see them as persons, and visit as friends in their homes, and know their hopes and anxieties, the fears of old age, and of sickness, the deep, deep God-hunger that is planted in them as in us all. Then Christ walks on the streets again. When, being at home among the great and comfortable, we count these starched respectabilities as things not to be grasped, but humble ourselves and take on ourselves the fashion of humble people, and being made humble as the humblest person by the leveling blindedness of love, we become obedient, even unto death. Yea, if it be His will, the death of a cross.

But the royal blindedness leads us also into stupendous ventures of faith. It set Paul and Barnabas, two lonely men, backed only by the goodwill of the Antioch church, to conquer the Mediterranean world for Christ. All rational calculations were against them. But blinded by Eternity within them, they saw no unconquerable obstacle in time. It set John Woolman, a humble tailor of New Jersey, to root out Negro slavery in this country. An absurd undertaking in 1750! But in 1800 every single slave owned by Quakers in Pennsylvania and New Jersey had been set free voluntarily, and the movement was rolling that issued in Abraham Lincoln and the Emancipation. Do you see war as a giant, iniquitous, futile, unchristian system? Then hurl yourself against it, in full blindness to the seeming impossibility of the task. For if God be for us, who can be against us? Does profit-seeking as the main stem of business strike you as the root of great evils? There are no impossibles to those who, in supreme dedication, are rooted deep in the Eternal Love. One shall overcome a thousand and two shall put ten thousand to flight, and the gates of hell shall not prevail against them. These are high words, but not lightly spoken. For creative, recreative, world-overturning living is possible when we as individuals and when the church as a fellowship become God-possessed channels through which the creative Love flows into the world of people. Serene, unhurried, undismayed, miraculous lives can be lived by you and by me, if we continuously will away the last vestige of claim upon ourselves and become wholly God-enthralled.

appendix

Reading Spiritual Classics for Personal and Group Formation

Many Christians today are searching for more spiritual depth, for something more than simply being good church members. That quest may send them to the spiritual practices of New Age movements or of Eastern religions such as Zen Buddhism. Christians, though, have their own long spiritual tradition, a tradition rich with wisdom, variety, and depth.

The great spiritual classics testify to that depth. They do not concern themselves with mystical flights for a spiritual elite. Rather, they contain very practical advice and insights that can support and shape the spiritual growth of any Christian. We can all benefit by sitting at the feet of the masters (both male and female) of Christian spirituality.

Reading spiritual classics is different from most of the reading we do. We have learned to read to master a text and extract information from it. We tend to read quickly, to get through a text. And we summarize as we read, seeking the main point. In reading spiritual classics, though, we allow the text to master and form us. Such formative reading goes more slowly, more reflectively, allowing time for God to speak to us through the text. God's word for us may come as easily from a minor point or even an aside as from the major point.

Formative reading requires that you approach

the text in humility. Read as a seeker, not as an expert. Don't demand that the text meet your expectations for what an "enlightened" author should write. Humility means accepting the author as another imperfect human, a product of his or her own time and situation. Learn to celebrate what is foundational in an author's writing without being overly disturbed by what is peculiar to the author's life and times. Trust the text as a gift from both God and the author, offered to you for your benefit—to help you grow in Christ.

To read formatively, you must also slow down. Feel free to reread a passage that seems to speak specially to you. Stop from time to time to reflect on what you have been reading. Keep a journal for these reflections. Often the act of writing can itself prompt further, deeper reflection. Keep your notebook open and your pencil in hand as you read. You might not get back to that wonderful insight later. Don't worry that you are not getting through an entire passage— or even the first paragraph! Formative reading is about depth rather than breadth, quality rather than quantity. As you read, seek God's direction for your own life. Timeless truths have their place but may not be what is most important for your own formation here and now.

As you read the passage, you might keep some of these questions running through your mind:

• How is what I'm reading true of my own life? Where does it reflect my own *experience*?

- How does this text challenge me? What new *direction* does it offer me?
- What must I change to put what I am reading into practice? How can I *incarnate* it, let this word become flesh in my life?

You might also devote special attention to sections that upset you. What is the source of the disturbance? Do you want to argue theology? Are you turned off by cultural differences? Or have you been skewered by an insight that would turn your life upside down if you took it seriously? Let your journal be a dialogue with the text.

If you find yourself moving from reading the text to chewing over its implications to praying, that's great! Spiritual reading is really the first step in an ancient way of prayer called *lectio divina* or "divine reading." Reading leads naturally into reflection on what you have read (meditation). As you reflect on what the text might mean for your life, you may well want to ask for God's help in living out any new insights or direction you have perceived (prayer). Sometimes such prayer may lead you further into silently abiding in God's presence (contemplation). And, of course, the process is only really completed when it begins to make a difference in the way we live (incarnation).

As good as it is to read spiritual classics in solitude, it is even better to join with others in a small group for mutual formation or "spiritual direction in common." This is *not* the same as a study group that talks *about* spiritual classics. A group for mutual formation would have similar goals as for an individual's reading: to allow the text to shine its light on the *experiences* of the group members, to suggest new *directions* for their lives and practical ways of *incarnating* these directions. Such a group might agree to focus on one short passage from a classic at each meeting (even if members have read more). Discussion usually goes much deeper if all the members have already read and reflected on the passage before the meeting and bring their journals.

Such groups need to watch for several potential problems. It is easy to go off on a tangent (especially if it takes the focus off the members' own experience and onto generalities). At such times a group leader might bring the group's attention back to the text: "What does our author say about that?" Or, "How do we experience that in our own lives?" When a group member shares a problem, others may be tempted to try to "fix" it. This is much less helpful than sharing similar experiences and how they were handled (for good or ill). "Sharing" someone else's problems (whether that person is in or out of the group) should be strongly discouraged.

One person could be designated as leader, to be responsible for opening and closing prayers; to be the first to share or respond to the text; and to keep notes during the discussion to highlight recurring themes, challenges, directives, or practical steps. These responsibilities could also be shared among several members of the group or rotated.

For further information about formative reading of spiritual classics, try *A Practical Guide to Spiritual Reading* by Susan Annette Muto. *Shaped by the Word* by Robert Mulholland (Upper Room Books) covers formative reading of the Bible. *Good Things Happen: Experiencing Community in Small Groups* by Dick Westley is an excellent resource on forming small groups of all kinds.